Dear Parent:
Your child's love of reading starts here!

Every child learns to read in a different way and at his or her own speed. Some go back and forth between reading levels and read favorite books again and again. Others read through each level in order. You can help your young reader improve and become more confident by encouraging his or her own interests and abilities. From books your child reads with you to the first books he or she reads alone, there are I Can Read Books for every stage of reading:

SHARED READING
Basic language, word repetition, and whimsical illustrations, ideal for sharing with your emergent reader

BEGINNING READING
Short sentences, familiar words, and simple concepts for children eager to read on their own

READING WITH HELP
Engaging stories, longer sentences, and language play for developing readers

READING ALONE
Complex plots, challenging vocabulary, and high-interest topics for the independent reader

ADVANCED READING
Short paragraphs, chapters, and exciting themes for the perfect bridge to chapter books

I Can Read Books have introduced children to the joy of reading since 1957. Featuring award-winning authors and illustrators and a fabulous cast of beloved characters, I Can Read Books set the standard for beginning readers.

A lifetime of discovery begins with the magical words **"I Can Read!"**

*Visit www.icanread.com for information
on enriching your child's reading experience.*

I Can Read Book® is a trademark of HarperCollins Publishers.

Mia Jazzes It Up!
Copyright © 2013 by HarperCollins Publishers
All Rights Reserved. Manufactured in China.
No part of this book may be used or reproduced in any manner whatsoever without written permission except in the case of brief quotations embodied in critical articles and reviews. For information address HarperCollins Children's Books, a division of HarperCollins Publishers, 195 Broadway, New York, NY 10007.
www.icanread.com
Book design by Sean Boggs
Library of Congress Catalog Card Number: 2013936297
ISBN 978-0-06-208692-1 (trade bdg.)—ISBN 978-0-06-208691-4 (pbk.)

16 17 SCP   10 9 8 7 6 5 4   ❖   First Edition

I Can Read!™ — SHARED My First READING

Mia
Jazzes It Up!

by Robin Farley
pictures by Aleksey and Olga Ivanov

HARPER
An Imprint of HarperCollinsPublishers

Today is a great day!

Mia is taking a new class.

She will learn jazz dance.

She packs her dance bag.

She takes out her ballet slippers.

She puts in her jazz shoes.

Mia's ballet slippers are pink.

They have pretty laces.

They are very fancy!

Mia's jazz shoes are black.

They are very plain.

At school, Mia changes
into her new dance clothes.
She slips on her new shoes.

Mia looks down at her feet.
She wishes her jazz shoes
were fancy like her slippers.

"Let's dance!"
sings Miss Bird.
"Follow me."

Miss Bird taps her feet.

The dancers tap their feet.

Miss Bird flaps her wings.

The dancers flap their arms.

Miss Bird spins around.

The dancers spin around, too.

They flap and tap and spin.
They dance together
until dance class is over.

"Do you like jazz dance?"
asks Mia's mom.

"I love it!" says Mia.
"Miss Bird makes
plain dance moves look jazzy!"

At home, Mia unpacks
her dance bag.
She looks at her jazz shoes.

They are nothing like jazz.
Mia thinks her plain shoes
should be as jazzy as dancing!

Mia has an idea!

She collects what she needs:

glue, sparkles, and ribbon.

Mia works hard.

Soon, the shoes are finished.

Mia cannot wait to wear them!

The next day, Mia skips
to dance school.
Her shoes sparkle in the sun.

Mia hopes her friends
will like her jazzy shoes.

Mia steps into her leotard.

She pulls on her dance skirt.

She saves her shoes for last.

"I love your shoes!"
says Ruby.
"Me, too!" says Bella.

Everyone loves

Mia's shoes!

Mia dances onto the floor.

"What lovely shoes!"
sings Miss Bird.
"Jazzy shoes for jazz dance!"

Mia smiles from ear to ear.

Her shoes are no longer plain.

They are jazzy!

31

Dictionary

Miss Bird's School of Dance

Ballet slippers

(you say it like this: ba-lay sli-purs)

The shoes worn by ballerinas

Jazz

(you say it like this: jaz) A type of dance that involves tap and shaking around

Leotard

(you say it like this: lee-uh-tard)

A piece of clothing dancers wear